HUMMEL ART

Price Guide
and
Supplement

By John F. Hotchkiss

HOW TO USE THIS SUPPLEMENT

The purpose of this *Price Guide and Supplement to Hummel Art* is to bring the basic book up to date. It is designed to be used in conjunction with *Hummel Art* and not intended to serve as a separate book. The old statement "A little knowledge is a dangerous thing" applies to this *Supplement*. The *Supplement* is not complete but contains only modifications of *Hummel Art*. Misconceptions and even grave errors could result from attempts to use this book alone without reference to the big book.

The reader should use the big book first. Then he should go to the corresponding section of the *Supplement* to determine if there is further information, especially when using the price lists. Although practically all prices have changed, these changes are not uniform in percentage or ratio to the prices in *Hummel Art*. Also, the column "Current Market Price" has been added because the actual prices many dealers are charging are significantly different from the "Suggested Retail Prices" issued by Goebel. Some of the reasons for these different prices are discussed further on.

This *Supplement* used in conjunction with *Hummel Art* should provide the reader with a useful resource to help him keep abreast of the fast moving and fascinating hobby of collecting Hummel art.

IMPORTANT

Be sure to read the important new information on reissues that were introduced by Goebel in 1978. The issue price of these later models is only a fraction of the price which was paid for almost identical ones with older marks because they were rare. Before buying any models listed in the Reissue Section be sure you appreciate the risks involved in buying examples with old marks and high prices or ones with new marks at several times their issue price. Goebel has given no indication of how many will be available in the years to come.

Copyright© 1979
John F. Hotchkiss

ISBN 0-87069-271-2
Library of Congress
Catalog Card No. 79-63079
Printed in U.S.A.

Third Printing, Revised 1979

Published by

Wallace-Homestead Book Company
1912 Grand Avenue
Des Moines, Iowa 50305

CONTENTS

REVISED PRICES IN TABLE A

The figures now shown in all five columns in Table A have been changed where advisable and now represent the maximum insurable values in dollars of examples in mint condition. Any collector that suffers an insurable loss should be able to find an equivalent replacement for the dollar values shown. Collectors making original acquisitions should be able to buy at these prices and even less from many authorized dealers. Collectors selling any pieces should expect to receive from 50% to 70% of the maximum insurable figures in Table A.

IDENTIFYING M.I. HUMMELS WILL NOW BE EASIER

All Hummel collectors will remember 1979 as the year when Goebel made two landmark changes, which, with each successive year, will become even more meaningful. It is hard to visualize any other two changes which would be of greater help in identifying and evaluating figurines and related articles.

For about thirty years the Goebel Company trademark has contained the figure of a bumble bee in at least eight variations. The word for bumble bee in German is "hummel." Since Goebel's most popular product line is adaptations of Sister Hummel's original works of art, a great many persons incorrectly assumed that anything marked with a bee was naturally a derivative of Sister Hummel's artwork. Unfortunately all of Goebel's other product lines, including such groups as Red Heads, Friar Tuck, and even Norman Rockwell carried exactly the same mark with the bee, so it was erroneously concluded that everything made by Goebel was a genuine M.I. Hummel product. Customers, salespersons, and even collectors were confused and in some cases inadvertantly misled.

The year 1979 should see the end of such confusion on new products. The Goebel Company has announced that during this year it will phase out all representations of the bee in the company trademark or logo. Only the word Goebel will identify the manufacturer. This new mark will be used on all products manufactured by them. The long familar "bee in the V" will be placed in the company archives after some thirty years of constant use and considerable confusion. From now on the only criteria for determining a genuine Hummel figurine will be the incised facsimile signature M.J.Hümmel on all but the tiniest of models. Because of size they will have only a label.

In recent years collectors have grouped all variations of the Goebel trademark into five categories for convenience. These classification are fully discussed in *Hummel Art*, pages 21 to 29, and form the five groups which indicate the approximate years of manufacture. The estimated value of any figurine is also related to which mark it has on the bottom. The new mark being introduced in 1979 will be referred to in the forthcoming book. *Hummel Art II*, as Trademark #6 (TMK-6) and probably will be nicknamed the "G" mark by collectors.

It is understood that the new mark will not be applied to the 1979 Annual Plate, #272—Singing Lesson or the 1979 Second Edition Annual Bell, #701—Farewell. The new mark as now planned will be used on these products starting with production of the 1980 versions. Since there is always the possibility of a slip between the cup and the lip, any such slips would make very interesting collectibles.

The second change that was introduced in January, 1979, is equally far-reaching. For the first time since the introduction of M.I. Hummel products in the 1930 s, each figurine or related article will carry the year of manufacture. Since 1935 admirers of these Hummel children have been discussing (and in some cases arguing heatedly) how to accurately determine the year any individual piece was made. For hundreds of thousands of collectors there has been no precise way of dating the year of manufacture. The trademark on the bottom of each piece has been the only rough and inaccurate date indicator available.

Other Hummel figures made during these forty some years have had a date incised or printed on the bottom which misled the majority of people into thinking it represented the year of manufacture. Actually it represented either the year of the "mother mold" or the year of the copyright, both closely associated. In one case figurines introduced for the first time in 1971 were incised with 1955 on the bottom. Nineteen fifty-five was the year they were copyrighted—**sixteen years** before they were released for sale!

For all future production, approximating the year will no longer be necessary. Starting in about January, 1979, when the master artist completes painting the face of a figurine he will not only apply his mark or initial in black with a fine brush on the base, but he will also add the current year right next to his mark. As the complete conversion is made this procedure should establish beyond all doubt the year any article was completed after 1978.

The impact that these two changes will have on collecting M.I. Hummel articles made before and after 1978 will not be fully felt for some time. There are many potential variations or production deviations that are almost certain to occur during the transition. Any irregularities are likely to become very desirable examples to collectors. From now on all M.I. Hummel figures marked with TMK-5 will be considered limited edition pieces. They will be limited to the quantities made prior to the trademark change and the painting of the year of manufacture on the bottom. Just how limited some of the models are will be of prime interest, concern, and speculation. The forthcoming book, *Hummel Art II*, will discuss some of the likely possibilities in much more detail.

TMK-1	TMK-2	TMK-3
CROWN MARK	**FULL BEE MARK**	**STYLIZED BEE MARK**
1935-1948	1950*-1959	1960*-65

*Dates are approximate — earlier documented examples are known.

FURTHER COMMENTS ON HUMMEL MARKS†

Documented evidence now exists that the trademarks TMK-2, TMK-3, and TMK-4 (see *Hummel Art*, page 22) were used by Goebel on an unknown limited number of figurines earlier than indicated by anything published to date. While more research is needed, examples of TMK-2 made before 1950 are known, as are TMK-3 marks in the 1950s, and TMK-4 marks before 1965. The importance of this information to collectors is now being evaluated.

A few examples of genuine M.J.Hummel figurines have been found without her mark. These are exceptions and must correspond in form and model number to the same one shown in the book. Buying the few examples of unmarked figurines and paying M. I. Hummel prices is best left to the experts.

Incised model numbers on the bottom of Goebel figurines that are preceded by one or more letters are the work of other Goebel artists, not those of Sister Hummel. During 1978 the Goebel Collectors' Club published a partial list of some of these other artists. For example, "Na" appearing as a prefix before a model number on the bottom of a figurine or other artistic work indicates having been created by Nasha, while "Rob" is on work created by Janet Robson. "Spö" is the abbreviation used on the work of Maria Spötl and "Stae" on that of Albert Staele. Even such illustrious American artists as Disney and Rockwell licensed some of their work to Goebel while Ispanky is one of the more recent noted sculptors to work for the company.

The fact that the letter H appears in the prefix does not indicate it is a Sister Hummel creation. This letter had several other uses in Goebel nomenclature. One of these, Hx 306/0/6, the Camel in the Nativity Set, merely means this is a religious figure other than a Madonna. Sister Hummel did not design this camel.

Hummel Art on page 24 shows the bases of two figurines with double crown marks; one is incised and one stamped in black ink in both illustrations 4. and 5. Double crown marks are infrequent and highly prized by collectors. Those fortunate enough to have examples of these early pieces should add a premium of 50 percent or more over the prices shown in the price column for single crown, TMK-1, when evaluating their collections.

The stamp on the bottom of figurines "U S Zone-Germany" indicates the piece was issued during part of 1946 or in 1947 or 1948. At the present time this additional marking does seem to command a premium price. And, as time goes on this should increase, as it has for other collectibles from Germany and Japan that are so marked.

Because of the great variety of combinations of marks and methods of application on Hummel articles, too much emphasis should not be reflected in pricing such deviations. At present too little is known about the significance or scarcity of such minor variations to assign them premium values. For example, at present there is interest on the part of some collectors as to whether or not the decal labels used since the late 1960s are applied under or overglaze. Since few details are available as to when or how many of a given model were labeled in one way or another, it seems unwise to convert such interest into dollars at this time.

TMK-4	TMK-5	TMK-6
THREE LINE MARK	**VEE/G MARK**	**G MARK**
©by W. Goebel W. Germany	Goebel	Goebel
1966*-1971	1972*-1979	1979-

†Note: The basic information on marks is contained on pages 21 through 29 of *Hummel Art*. Familiarity with this material is a prerequisite to the information that follows.

READER COMMENTS
ON *HUMMEL ART*

"I have been collecting and enjoying Hummels for at least 30 years. In my opinion *Hummel Art* is one of the best and most complete books on Hummels that I have had the pleasure to enjoy."

A. T.
North Arlington, N.J.

"Your book *Hummel Art* is, in my opinion, a must for all Hummel collectors. My days of research are over. I can now turn to *Hummel Art* for the many questions that arise regarding my collection—markings, repairs, etc. I now have them all at my fingertips in one book. It has been a valuable asset in my efforts to identify my Hummels and to place a value on my collection."

D. H.
Andrews AFB, Maryland

"Just wanted to let you know how much I have enjoyed your *Hummel Art* book. I am rather new at Hummel collecting and have practically worn out the pages in your volume reading and re-reading about my new interest and love."

M. B.
Clarksburg, W.Va.

"I have thoroughly enjoyed reading and studying your book on *Hummel Art*. It is perhaps the best source which I have found to date and is an excellent piece of work."

R. C.
Millersville, Maryland

"Let me say how very much we enjoy and use your reference book on Hummels. I recommend it to all our collector customers."

D. O.
Tacoma, Wash.

"A thousand compliments and thanks for your excellent *Hummel Art* book! I received the book as a Christmas gift, and it has more than answered all the questions I had concerning Hummel figurines. In fact, it was all so satisfactory I felt I had to drop you a line and tell you that you helped a small collector of small means a very great deal!"

M. O.
Meriden, Conn.

"After purchasing your book *Hummel Art*, which is highly informative and interesting, I realized that I have a number of old and very valuable figurines."

R. C.
Kennebunk, Maine

"I would like to congratulate you on your new book *Hummel Art*. As both a collector and dealer I've been waiting for such a book to appear. I'm so glad you decided to do it."

J. T.
Manchester, Washington

"I purchased your book at Christmas. I think I got it because even though I cannot afford all those figurines, this is one way I can enjoy them."

C. E.
Cincinnati, Ohio

CURRENT
M. I. HUMMEL FIGURINES
AND ADAPTATIONS

The following photographs are an alphabetical listing of Hummel figures currently being produced by Goebel. Figures not photographed are cross-referenced.

Figurines

A FAIR MEASURE
Hummel, 345

2. ACCORDION BOY
Hummel, 185

3. ADORATION
Hummel, 23

4. ADVENTURE BOUND
Hummel, 347

ANGEL DUET
Hum. 261.
See Angel Duet, Candleholder,
Hum. 193

ANGEL SERENADE
Hum. 214/D.
See Nativity Set for picture. Angel
Serenade (standing) Hum. 83 is
discontinued. See Section II, Table
II.

ANGEL TRIO (A)
Hum. III 38/0, 39/0, 40/0.
See Angel Trio (A) in
Candleholders.

ANGEL TRIO (B)
Hum. 238/A-C.
See Angel Trio (B) in Candleholders
for picture.

ANGEL WITH ACCORDION
Hum. 238/B.
See Angel Trio (B), in
Candleholders for picture.

ANGEL WITH LUTE
Hum. 238/8.
See Angel Trio (B), Candleholders,
for picture.

ANGELIC SLEEP
Hum. 25.
See Candleholders for picture.

5. ANGELIC CARE
Hummel, 194

6. ANGELIC SONG
Hummel, 144

7. APPLE TREE BOY
Hummel, 142

8. APPLE TREE GIRL
Hummel, 141

9. ARTIST, THE
Hummel, 304

10. AUF WIEDERSEHEN
Hummel, 153

11. AUTUMN HARVEST
Hummel, 355

12. BAKER
Hummel, 128

13. BAND LEADER
Hummel, 129

14. BARNYARD HERO
Hummel, 195

15. BASHFUL
Hummel, 377

16. BE PATIENT
Hummel, 197

17. BEGGING HIS SHARE
Hummel, 9

18. BIG HOUSE-CLEANING
Hummel, 363

19. BIRD DUET
Hummel, 169

20. BIRTHDAY SERENADE
Hummel, 218

21. BLESSED EVENT
Hummel, 333

22. BOOK WORM
Hummel 3; Hummel 8

BOY WITH ACCORDION
Hum. 390.
See Children Trio (B) for picture.

BOY WITH HORSE
Hum. 117.
See Christmas Angels in
Candleholders for picture.

BOY WITH HORSE
Hum. 239/C.
See Children Trio (A) for picture.

23.   BOOTS
Hummel, 143

24.   BOY WITH TOOTHACHE
Hummel, 217

25.   BROTHER
Hummel, 95

26.   BUILDER, THE
Hummel, 305

27.   BUSY STUDENT
Hummel, 367

28.   CARNIVAL
Hummel, 328

29.   CELESTIAL MUSICIAN
Hummel, 188

30.   CHICK GIRL
Hummel, 57

31. CHICKEN-LICKEN
Hummel, 385

32. CHILDREN TRIO (A)
Hummel, 239/A, 239/B, 239/C

33. CHILDREN TRIO (B)
Hummel, 389, 390, 391

34. CHIMNEY SWEEP
Hummel, 12

5. CHRIST CHILD
ummel, 18

36. CINDERELLA
Hummel, 337

37. CLOSE HARMONY
Hummel, 336

38. CONFIDENTIALLY
Hummel, 314

39. CONGRATULATIONS
Hummel, 17

40. COQUETTES
Hummel, 179

41. CROSSROADS
Hummel, 331

42. CULPRITS
Hummel, 56/A

43. DOCTOR
Hummel, 127

44. DOLL BATH
Hummel, 319

45. DOLL MOTHER
Hummel, 67

46. DRUMMER
Hummel, 240

47. DUET
Hummel, 130

48. EASTER GREETINGS
Hummel, 378

49. EASTER TIME
Hummel, 384

EASTER PLAYMATES (secondary name for Hum. 384).

50. EVENTIDE
Hummel, 99

51. FAREWELL
Hummel, 65

52. FARM BOY
Hummel, 66

53. FAVORITE PET
Hummel, 361

54. FEATHERED FRIENDS
Hummel, 344

55. FEEDING TIME
Hummel, 199

13

58. FLOWER VENDOR
Hummel, 381

56. FESTIVAL HARMONY (MANDOLIN) 57. FESTIVAL HARMONY (FLUTE)
Hummel, 172   Hummel, 173

59. FLYING ANGEL
Hummel, 366

60. FOLLOW THE LEADER
Hummel, 369

61. FOR FATHER
Hummel, 87

62. FOR MOTHER
Hummel, 257

63. FRIENDS
Hummel, 136

64. GAY ADVENTURE
Hummel, 356

GIRL WITH DOLL
HUM. 239/B.
See Children Trio (A) for picture.

GIRL WITH FIR TREE
Hum. 116.
See Christmas Angels,
Candleholders.

GIRL WITH NOSEGAY
Hum. 115.
See Christmas Angels,
Candleholders.

GIRL WITH NOSEGAY
Hum. 239/A.
See Children Trio (A) for picture.

GIRL WITH SHEET OF MUSIC
Hum. 389.
See Children Trio (B) for picture.

GIRL WITH TRUMPET
Hum. 391.
See Children Trio (B) for picture.

65.   GLOBE TROTTER
Hummel, 79

66.   GOING TO GRANDMA'S
Hummel, 52

67.   GOOD FRIENDS
Hummel, 182

68.   GOOD HUNTING!
Hummel, 307

69.   GOOD NIGHT
Hummel, 214/C

70.   GOOD SHEPHERD
Hummel, 42

71.   GOOSE GIRL
Hummel, 47

15

72. GUIDING ANGEL
Hummel, 357

73. HAPPINESS
Hummel, 86

74. HAPPY BIRTHDAY
Hummel, 176

75. HAPPY DAYS
Hummel, 150

76. HAPPY PASTIME
Hummel, 69

77. HAPPY TRAVELLER
Hummel, 109

HEAVENLY LULLABY
Hum. 262.
See Lullaby Heavenly, Hum. 262

78. HEAR YE, HEAR YE
Hummel, 15

79. HEAVENLY ANGEL
Hummel, 21

80. HEAVENLY PROTECTION
Hummel, 88

81. HELLO
Hummel, 124

82. THE HOLY CHILD
Hummel, 70

83. HOME FROM MARKET
Hummel, 198

84. HOMEWARD BOUND
Hummel, 334

HOLY FAMILY
Hum. 214/A, 214/B.
See Nativity for picture.

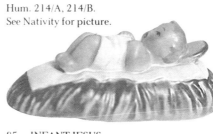

85. INFANT JESUS
Hummel, 214/A/K

86. INFANT OF KRUMBAD
Hummel, 78/III

87. JOYFUL
Hummel, 53

JOYFUL ADVENTURE
Hum. 356. See Gay Adventure for picture.

88. JUST RESTING
Hummel, 112

89. KISS ME
Hummel, 311

90. KNITTING LESSON
Hummel, 256

17

91. LATEST NEWS
Hummel, 184

92. LET'S SING
Hummel, 110

93. LETTER TO SANTA CLAUS
Hummel, 340

94. LITTLE BAND (on base)
Hummel, 392

95. LITTLE BOOKKEEPER
Hummel, 306

96. LITTLE CELLIST
Hummel, 89

97. LITTLE FIDDLER
Hummel 2, 4

98. LITTLE GABRIEL
Hummel, 32

99. LITTLE GARDENER
Hummel, 74

00. LITTLE GOAT HERDER
Hummel, 200

101. LITTLE GUARDIAN
Hummel, 145

102. LITTLE HELPER
Hummel, 73

03. LITTLE HIKER
Hummel, 16

104. LITTLE PHARMACIST
Hummel, 322

105. LITTLE SCHOLAR
Hummel, 80

06. LITTLE SHOPPER
Hummel, 96

107. LITTLE SWEEPER
Hummel, 171

108. LITTLE TAILOR
Hummel, 308

109. LITTLE THRIFTY
Hummel, 118

110. BASE, LITTLE THRIFTY
Showing door and key

111. LITTLE TOOTER
(Shepherd Kneeling with Flute)
Hummel, 214/H

112. LOST SHEEP, THE
Hummel, 68

113. LOST STOCKING
Hummel, 374

114. LULLABY, HEAVENLY
Hummel, 262

115. MAIL IS HERE
(Mail Coach)
Hummel, 226

116. MARCH WINDS
Hummel, 43

117. MAX AND MORITZ
Hummel, 123

118. MEDITATION
Hummel, 13

119. MERRY WANDERER
Hummel 7, 11

120. MISCHIEF MAKER
Hummel, 342

121. MOTHER'S DARLING
Hummel, 175

122. MOTHER'S HELPER
Hummel, 133

123. MOUNTAINEER
Hummel, 315

124. NOT FOR YOU!
Hummel, 317

125. ON SECRET PATH
Hummel, 386

126. OUT OF DANGER
Hummel, 56/B

21

127. PHOTOGRAPHER, THE
Hummel, 178

128. PLAYMATES
Hummel, 58

129. POSTMAN
Hummel, 119

130. PRAYER BEFORE BATTLE
Hummel, 20

131. PUPPY LOVE
Hummel, 1

132. RETREAT TO SAFETY
Hummel, 201

133. RIDE INTO CHRISTMAS
Hummel, 396

134. RING AROUND THE
ROSIE   Hummel, 348

135. RUNAWAY, THE
Hummel, 327

136. ST. GEORGE
Hummel, 55

137. ST. JOSEPH
Hummel, 214/B

138. SCHOOL BOY
Hummel, 82

139. SCHOOL BOYS
Hummel, 170

140. SCHOOL GIRL
Hummel, 81

141. SCHOOL GIRLS
Hummel, 177

142. SENSITIVE HUNTER
Hummel, 6

143. SERENADE
Hummel, 85

144. SHEPHERD'S BOY
Hummel, 64

145. SHE LOVES ME,
SHE LOVES ME NOT!
Hummel, 174

SHEPHERD KNEELING WITH
FLUTE
Hum. 214/H/II.
See Little Tooter.

146. SHINING LIGHT
Hummel, 358

147. SIGNS OF SPRING
Hummel, 203

148. SINGING LESSON
Hummel, 63

149. SISTER
Hummel, 98

150. SKIER
Hummel, 59

151. SMART LITTLE SISTER, THE
Hummel, 346

152. SOLDIER BOY
Hummel, 332

153. SOLOIST
Hummel, 135

154. SPRING CHEER
Hummel, 72

155. SPRING DANCE
Hummel, 353

156. STARGAZER
Hummel, 132

157. STITCH IN TIME, A
Hummel, 255

158. STORMY WEATHER
Hummel, 71

159. STREET SINGER
Hummel, 131

160. STROLLING ALONG
Hummel, 5

161. SURPRISE
Hummel, 94

162. SWEET MUSIC
Hummel, 186

THE RUNAWAY
Hum. 327
See Runaway, The for picture.

163.   TELLING HER SECRET
Hummel, 196

164.   TO MARKET
Hummel, 49

165.   TRUMPET BOY
Hummel, 97

166.   TUNEFUL ANGEL
Hummel, 359

167.   UMBRELLA BOY
Hummel, 152/A

168.   UMBRELLA GIRL
Hummel, 152/B

169.   VALENTINE GIFT
Hummel, 387
(See Goebel Collectors' Club.)

170.   VILLAGE BOY
Hummel, 51

171.   VISITING AN INVALID
Hummel, 382

172. VOLUNTEERS
Hummel, 50

173. WAITER
Hummel, 154

174. WASH DAY
Hummel, 321

WATCHFUL ANGEL
Hum. 194. See Angelic Care.

175. WAYSIDE DEVOTION
Hummel, 28

176. WAYSIDE HARMONY
Hummel, 111

177. WEARY WANDERER
Hummel, 204

178. WE CONGRATULATE
Hummel, 220 (if no base # is 214/E)

179. WHICH HAND?
Hummel, 258

180. WHITSUNTIDE
Hummel, 163 (Reissued, 1978)

Ashtrays

183. HAPPY PASTIME
Hummel, 62

181. WORSHIP
Hummel, 84

182. BOY WITH BIRD
Hummel, 166

185. LET'S SING
Hummel, 114

186. SINGING LESSON
Hummel, 34

184. JOYFUL
Hummel, 33

Bells

First Annual Hummel Bell. LET'S SING!
Hummel, 700.

Second Annual Hummel Bell. FAREWELL
Hummel, 701.

Bookends

187. APPLE TREE BOY AND GIRL
Hummel, 252/A + B

188. BOOKWORM
Hummel, 14/A + B

189. GOOSE GIRL AND FARM BOY
Hummel, 60/A + B

190. LITTLE GOAT HERDER
AND FEEDING TIME
Hummel, 250/A + B

191. PLAYMATES AND CHICK GIRL
Hummel, 61/A + B

Candleholders

ADVENT CANDLESTICKS,
Hum. No's 115, 116, 117,
see Christmas Angels for pictures.

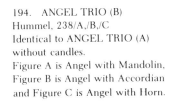

193. ANGEL TRIO (A)
Hummel, III/40,/38,/39

194. ANGEL TRIO (B)
Hummel, 238/A,/B,/C
Identical to ANGEL TRIO (A)
without candles.
Figure A is Angel with Mandolin,
Figure B is Angel with Accordian
and Figure C is Angel with Horn.

192. ANGEL DUET
Hummel, 193

195. ANGELIC SLEEP
Hummel, 25

196. CANDLELIGHT
Hummel, 192

197. CHRISTMAS ANGELS (SET)
Hummel, 117, 115, 116

198. HERALD ANGELS
Hummel, 37

199.   LITTLE BAND
Hummel, 388

200.   LULLABY
Hummel, 24

201.   SILENT NIGHT
Hummel, 54

NOTE: Illustrations of Candy Boxes, Fonts, and Lamps have
        been omitted as similar figures are shown as figurines.

Madonnas

229.   FLOWER MADONNA
Hummel, 10

MADONNA (Kneeling)
See Nativity Set 260, for picture.

230.   MADONNA WITH HALO
Hummel, 45

231.   MADONNA WITHOUT
HALO
Hummel, 46

Music Boxes

232. LITTLE BAND (with candle)
Hummel, 388/M

233. LITTLE BAND
Hummel, 392/M

Nativity Sets

234. SMALL NATIVITY SET
Hummel, 214 A-0 + 366

235. LARGE NATIVITY SET
Hummel, 260 A-R

Plaques

236. BA-BEE RING
Hummel, 30/A

237. Back of ring
showing signature

238. CHILD IN BED
Hummel 48

239. LITTLE FIDDLER
Hummel, 93
(Discontinued)

240. MADONNA
Hummel, 48

241. MAIL IS HERE (Mail Coach)
Hummel, 140

242. MERRY WANDERER
Hummel, 92
(Reinstated, 77)

244. QUARTET
Hummel, 134

245. RETREAT TO SAFETY
Hummel, 126

246. VACATION TIME
Hummel, 125

33

Annual Plates

247. ANNUAL PLATE—1971
Heavenly Angel, Hum. 264

248. ANNUAL PLATE—1972
Hear Ye, Hear Ye, Hum. 265

249. ANNUAL PLATE—1973
Globetrotter, Hum. 266

250. ANNUAL PLATE—1974
Goose Girl, Hum. 267

251. ANNUAL PLATE—1975
Ride into Christmas, Hum. 268

252. ANNUAL PLATE—1976
Apple Tree Girl, Hum. 269

253. ANNUAL PLATE—1977
Apple Tree Boy, Hum. 270

254. ANNUAL PLATE—1978
Happy Pastime, Hum. 271

255. ANNUAL PLATE—1979
Singing Lesson, Hum. 272

256. ANNIVERSARY PLATE—1975
Stormy Weather, Hum. 280

Miscellaneous

257. M.I. HUMMEL BUST   (OLD)
Hummel, HU 1

258. SISTER M.I. HUMMEL BUST
Hummel, HU 2

259. Base of Hu 1 showing
sculptor's signature
(Skrobek) and date (1965)

SPECIAL NOTE ON BELLS

1980 to 1990
Figurine models reportedly selected for use on
Annual Bells are as follows:

Name	Hum. No.
Bookworm	3
Joyful	53
Good Friends	182
Latest News	184
Little Bookkeeper	306
Cinderella	337
Smart Little Sister	346
Favorite Pet	361
Big Housecleaning	363
Busy Student	367

These figures may not appear in the sequence listed and changes may be made in model subjects.

HELP WANTED:

Hummel collectors and dealers for contributions to other Hummel enthusiasts of information you would like added, changed or deleted in this Supplement or in a new edition of HUMMEL ART to be published soon. Give others the benefit of your expertise and knowledge and you can benefit from theirs. Send your ideas, facts, and pictures which other Hummel owners will enjoy to:

John F. Hotchkiss,
306 Bay Village Drive
Rochester, NY 14609

PRICES OF
HUMMEL FIGURINES
TABLE A

The January, 1978, prices in the first edition of *Hummel Art* have changed in a surprising degree. The prices in this *Supplement* reflect these changes and supersede them. For easy reference Tables I through IV, pages 33 to 142 in *Hummel Art* have been combined into one Table A in this *Supplement*. This table is arranged in numerical order while the pictures and names just preceding Table A are in alphabetical order. There are about six thousand new prices given and additional related information supplied which completely updates *Hummel Art*.

In Table A, prices listed under TMK-5 (the 1972-79 production trademark) are taken directly from the January, 1979, Goebel U.S.A. price list. They are manufacturer's "Suggested Retail Price" which the company recommends dealers charge their retail customers. The CMP column ("Current Market Price") is new to our readers as it did not appear in *Hummel Art*. It is our best estimate of the *actual average price* dealers are charging and getting for that item. The "Current Market Price" column appears adjacent to the "Suggested Retail Price" column so that the reader can compare these two sets of figures. Those items whose current market prices are most widely divergent from the suggested retail are the Reissues shown on separate Table B on page 55 and those figurines which match one of the Annual Plates or Bells.

Prices of figures with older marks (TMK-1, 2, 3, and 4) also appear in Table A in correspondingly named columns. While some old mark prices advanced at a slower pace than those of some new figurines, others, such as the 1971 Annual Plate, soared, leading the parade. New discoveries of old mark figurines are indicated by showing a price, where in *Hummel Art* there was a "?" or an "a". All narrative information in Table A modifies information in *Hummel Art*.

The synthesis of about fifteen thousand prices obtained by dealers from around the United States and paid at auctions appears as the realistic Current Market Prices as of January, 1979. A great many of these are 50 percent or more above those published in *Hummel Art* just one year ago. This increase is not only astounding but also an unrealistic indication of what may be expected in the future if Hummel collecting is going to remain enjoyable and practical.

There are many items that escalated more than 50 percent during 1978. As would be expected these were cases where for a number of reasons the demand outdistanced the "visible" supply. A good example is the 1978 Annual Plate which was issued in January at the suggested retail price of $65. By June, these plates were being sold in the secondary market for about $275. The first Annual Bell was issued at $50 with prices running as high as $300 in June. By the end of the year additional effort and publicity by the Goebel Company helped to drop the price of the plate to about $140 and the price of the bell to about $160 in some cases. Wide variations of these prices exist from dealer to dealer.

It is interesting to note that many dealers and most department stores with real concern for their longtime customers continued to sell whatever was allocated to them at regular prices on a first come or "want list" basis. This exemplary policy certainly won well deserved applause from the recipients.

Many questions are being asked about what's going to happen in 1979 and later. Is there going to be a repeat of 1978? It would be much easier for economists to make an intelligent prediction of the trend of interest rates or for anyone to forecast the direction of the economy in 1979 than it would to attempt to answer these questions correctly. Therefore, it is urged that you buy available examples if you like them and can afford them, but under no circumstances make the purchase with the idea that it is an investment on which you are going to realize a profit.

TABLE A
MASTER NUMERICAL PRICE LIST
M. I. HUMMEL FIGURINES

Key To Symbols:

AT—Ashtray; BE—Bookends; BL—Bell; CBX—Candy Box;CAN—Candleholders; F—Figurines; HWF—Font, Holy Water; MAD—Madonna; NAT—Nativity (or piece); PLT—Nativity Set (or piece); PLT—Plate; PLQ—Plaque; MBX—Music Box; TLP—Table Lamp base; WVS—Wall Vase.

A—Assigned; C—Cancelled; D—Disontinued; O—Open; P—Produced; NA—Not Available; R—Reissued; "—" Not Known with This Mark; "?"—Availability not verified.

Column headed $\frac{TMK}{5}$ contains Suggested U.S. Retail Prices (SRP) by Goebel.

CMP—Current Market Price.

Number/ Size Mark	Name	Size	Status	TMK-1 Crown	TMK-2 Full Bee	TMK-3 Styl. Bee	TMK-4 3/Line	TMK-5 V/Gee
1	PUPPY LOVE	4½"	P	260	190	120	95	85
	Change HUM. ART, p.118 to 5".							
2/0	LITTLE FIDDLER	6"	P	300	225	140	110	90
/I		7½"	P	?	550	350	300	200
/II		10¾"	P	?	1,300	900	750	600
/III		12¼"	R	2,000	1,500	1200	–	1,000
3/I	BOOKWORM	5½"	P	500	400	250	200	165
/II		8"	P	1250	850	700	600	600
/III				–	2,500	1,800	?	1,000
4	LITTLE FIDDLER	4¾"	P	250	180	110	85	75
	Found w/TMK-2 (5½") add 25%.							
5	STROLLING ALONG	4¾"	P	220	160	100	85	75
6/0	SENSITIVE HUNTER	4¾"	P	250	190	110	85	75
/I		5½"	P	280	200	140	110	90
/II		7½"	P	500	400	290	225	210
	See HUM. ART, p.111 for variations.							
7/0	MERRY WANDERER	6¼"	P	300	250	165	130	115
/I		7"	P	700	525	325	250	210
/II		9½"	P	2,000	1,500	1,000	800	600
/III		11¼"	R	3,500	2,500	1,800	?	1,000
/X		29"	P	–	–	–	–	11,000
	See HUM. ART, p.91 for variations. Not in 1979 Goebel catalog.							
8	BOOKWORM	4"	P	300	225	140	100	85
9	BEGGING HIS SHARE	5½"	P	300	225	140	100	90
	See HUM. ART, p.107.							
10/I/11	FLOWER MADONNA	8¼"	P	–	350	215	170	140
/I/W		8¼"	P	240	180	110	90	80
/II/11		?	D?					
/II/W		?	D?					
/III/11		11½"	P	1,350	1,000	630	500	325
	Reported w/ 10/3. Add 20%.							
/III/W		11½"	P	?	500	300	250	185
11/2/0	MERRY WANDERER	4¼"	P	180	135	85	65	55
/0		4¾"	P	200	150	110	90	80
—		5½"	D	250	175	–	–	NA

Number/ Size Mark	Name	Size	Status	TMK-1 Crown	TMK-2 Full Bee	TMK-3 Styl. Bee	TMK-4 3/Line	TMK-5 V/Gee
12/2/0	CHIMNEY SWEEP	4″	P	150	100	60	48	50
/0		?	D?	?	?	?	?	
12		6¼″	D	450	300	—	—	
/I		5½″	P	240	180	110	90	80
/II		7″	D					
13/2/0	MEDITATION	4½″	P	?	?	85	65	60
/0		5½″	P	450*	300	110	90	85
/I	*For oversize only	?	D?					
/II		7″	R	2,500	2000	1500	1200	400
/III		?	D?	?	?	?	?	
/IV		?	D?	?	?	?	?	
/V		13¾″	R	–	5,000	3,500	2000	1,500
14/A&B BE	Bookworms Sold only ar pair. No separate boy figurine	5½″	P	500	400	250	200	185
15/0	HEAR YE, HEAR YE	5″	P	280	210	130	110	90
	Note: Crown & Full Bee examples — tip of spear is baby-blue not gray.							
/I		6″	P	380	285	175	140	130
/II		8¾″	P	?	?	340	270	225
16/2/0	LITTLE HIKER	4½″	P	150	100	70	55	50
/0		?	D?					
/I		6″	P	200	150	110	90	80
17/0	CONGRATULATONS	6″		?	150	125	72	80
	See HUM. ART, p.108 for variations.							
/I		?	D					
/II		8″	D					
18	CHRIST CHILD	6″ × 2″	P	220	165	100	80	70
19	(UNKNOWN)	?	C					
20	PRAYER BEFORE BATTLE	4½″	P	280	160	130	100	85
21/0	HEAVENLY ANGEL	4¾″	P	180	135	85	65	70
/0/½		6″	P	265	200	120	95	85
/I		6¾″	P	345	260	160	125	110
/II		8¾″	P	650	475	325	200	200
22/0 HWF	Angel with Birds *Reclassified from HUM. ART "D".*	2¾″ × 3½″	P*	70	50	31	25	20
/I		3¼″ × 4″	D	?	120	85	?	NA
23/I	ADORATION	6¼″	P	550	400	260	200	175
/II		7¾″	D	?	*	?	?	
	Found as 23/2, TMK-2. Previously unlisted, low 4-digit figure price.							
/III		9″	P*			350	290	250
	Prev. listing of "D" changed to "P".							
24/I CAN	Lullaby	5″ × 3½″	P	300	230	140	110	90
/II		?	D?					
/III		6″ × 8¾″	R	3,000	2,500	2,000	?	575
	HUM. ART, p.49, Illus.114 is HEAVENLY LULLABY, 262.							
25	ANGELIC SLEEP	3½″ × 5″	D?					
/I		5″ × 3½″	P	300	225	140	100	105
26/0 HWF	Child Jesus	1½″ × 5″	P	60	50	30	23	90
/I		2½″ × 6″	D	?	120	75	50	NA
27/I	JOYOUS NEWS	?	D?					NA
/II		?	D?					
/III		4½″ × 4¼″	R*	2,000	1,500	1,000		350
	Scarce in U.S.A.							

Number/ Size Mark	Name	Size	Status	TMK-1 Crown	TMK-2 Full Bee	TMK-3 Styl. Bee	TMK-4 3/Line	TMK-5 V/Gee
28/I	WAYSIDE DEVOTION	?	D?					
/II		7½"	P	550	400	280	220	180
/III		8¾"	P	700	500	325	250	250
29/0 HWF	Guardian Angel	2½" × 6"	D	?	?	?	?	NA
30/A&B PLQ	Ba-Bee Rings (2)	4¾" × 5"	P	300	240	150	115	95
	Models w/red rings rare, $600±.							
31 CAN	Advent Group with Candle	4¾" × 3¾"	D?	?	?	?	?	NA
	One black child—one example known, mid 4-digit.							
32	LITTLE GABRIEL	5"	P	190	145	85	70	60
33 AT	Joyful	3½" × 6"	P	?	170	100	80	60
34 AT	Singing Lesson	3½" × 6¼"	P	?	230	140	110	75
35/0 HWF	Good Shepherd	2¼" × 4¾"	P	50	35	25	22	50
	See HUM. ART, p.109 for more details.							
/I		2¾" × 5¾"	D	?	?	?	?	NA
36/0 HWF	Angel with Flowers	2¾" × 4"	P	50	40	24	19	20
/I		3½" × 4½"	D	?	?	?	?	NA
37 CAN	Herald Angels	4" × 2¼"	P	300	225	140	100	85
III/38/0 CAN	Angel, Joyous News w/Lute	2"	P	250	190	115	90	80
/I		2¾"	D	?	?	?	?	NA
	Prices for set of 3, sold singly.							
III/39/0 CAN	Angel, Joyous News w/Accordion	2"	P	250	190	115	90	80
/I	Little Advent Angels w/Concertina	2¾"	D	?	?	?	?	NA
	Prices for set of 3, sold singly.							
III/40/0 CAN	Angel, Joyous News w/Trumpet	2"	P	250	190	115	90	80
/I	Little Advent Angel w/Trumpet	2¾"	D	?	?	?	?	NA
	Note: Sold as one of set of 3—price is for set.							
41	(UNKNOWN)	?	C					
42	GOOD SHEPHERD	6¼"	P	250	175	120	95	75
/I		7½"	D	–	300	–	–	NA
	Listed in HUM. ART as 8".							
43	MARCH WINDS	5"	P	180	135	80	65	70
M44/A TLP	Culprits	9½"	P	?	550	340	270	220
/B TLP	Out of Danger	9½"	P	740	550	340	270	220
45/0/6 MAD	MADONNA WITH HALO	10½"	P	150	100	80	60	40
/0/13		10½"	D	?	?	90	75	NA
/0/W		10½"	P	–	?	45	35	25
/I/6		12"	R	?	?	?	?	55
I/W		12"	P	?	?	?	?	35
/II/6			D?	?	?	?	?	NA
/II/W			D?	?	?	?	?	NA
/III/6		16¾"	R	?	?	150	?	100
/III/W		16¾"	R	?	?	?	?	70

Number/ Size Mark	Name	Size	Status	TMK-1 Crown	TMK-2 Full Bee	TMK-3 Styl. Bee	TMK-4 3/Line	TMK-5 V/Gee
46/0/6 MAD	MADONNA, PRAYING *Also called Madonna w/o Halo.*	10¼″	P	?	?	75	60	40
/0/13		10½″	D	?	?	100	75	NA
/0/W		10¼″	P	?	?	45	35	25
/I/6		11¼″	D	?	?	?	?	60
/I/13		11½″	D	?	?	?	?	NA
/I/W		11¼″	P	?	100	60	48	30
/III/6		16¾″	R	–	–	–	–	125
/III/13		16¾″	D	?	?	?	?	NA
/III/W		16¾″	R	–	–	–	–	100
47/3/0	GOOSE GIRL	4″	P	?	180	110	90	25
/2/0		?	D?					
/0		4¾″	P	300	225	140	100	95
/II		7½″	P	600	500	370	290	240
48/0 PLQ	Madonna	3″ × 4″	P	180	135	85	65	50
/II		4¾″ × 6″	R	400	300	200	?	150
	(w/metal frame)	–						
/V		8½″ × 10″	D	1,000	850	?	?	NA
	(without metal frame)							
49/3/0	TO MARKET	4″	P	275	200	120	95	80
/2/0		?	D	?	?	?	?	NA
	See HUM. ART, p.121. Rare w/TMK-1.							
49/0	TO MARKET (Cont'd) *See HUM. ART, p.121. Rare w/TMK-1.*	5½″	P	350	250	175	140	100
/I		6¼″	R	?	?	?	?	250
50/2/0	VOLUNTEERS	5″	P	?	270	166	130	125
/0		5½″	R	700	550	?	?	170
/I		6½″	R	1,000	800	?	?	250
51/3/0	VILLAGE BOY	4″	P	140	100	65	50	50
/2/0		5¼″	P	200	150	100	80	60
/0		6″	P	250	200	120	95	80
/I		7¼″	R	800	600	500	–	190
52/0	GOING TO GRANDMA'S	4¾″	P	320	240	150	115	100
–		?	D	900	?	?	?	NA
/I		6″	R	1,000	800	500	–	250
	Delete 1950 name, p.121.							
53	JOYFUL *Called "Banjo Betty" in 1950.*	4″	P	210	150	65	50	55
III/53 CBX		6¼″	P	?	?	160	125	95
54 CAN	Silent Night *Delete remarks, p.112, add to 31.*	4¾″ × 3¾″	P	?	285	185	145	110
55	SAINT GEORGE	6¾″	P	400	300	250	200	165
56/A	CULPRITS *TMK-2 reported 7″ high, add 20%.*	6¼″	P	?	240	150	116	110
56/B	OUT OF DANGER *TMK-2 reported 7″ high, add 20%.*	6¼″	P	320	240	150	116	110
57/0	CHICK GIRL	3½″	P	200	150	90	70	90
/I		4¼″	P	300	225	150	120	120
III/57 CBX	Chick Girl	6¼″	P	300	225	150	120	95
58/0	PLAYMATES	4″	P	200	150	90	70	90
/I		4¼″	P	300	225	160	120	125
III/58 CBX	Playmates	6¼″	P	?	?	160	120	95

Number/ Size Mark	Name	Size	Status	TMK-1 Crown	TMK-2 Full Bee	TMK-3 Styl. Bee	TMK-4 3/Line	TMK-5 V/Gee
59	SKIER	5″	P	300	240	120	95	95
	See HUM. ART, p.112 for variations.							
60/A&B BE	Farm Boy & Goose Girl	4¾″	P	600	450	315	250	180
	Note: Prices for pairs, only.							
61/A&B BE	Playmates & Chick Girl	4″	P	600	450	315	250	180
	Prices for pairs, only.							
62 AT	Happy Pastime	3½″ × 6¼″	P	250	175	120	95	75
63	SINGING LESSON	2¾″	P	300	220	150	100	125
	This figure appears on 1979 plate. Double crown reported, add 50%.							
III/63 CBX	Singing Lesson	6″	P	?	?	160	125	100
64	SHEPHERD'S BOY	5½″	P	280	210	130	100	90
65	FAREWELL	4¾″	P	340	255	160	125	130
	Reported marked 65/I—add 25%.							
66	FARM BOY	5″	P	270	200	125	100	90
67	DOLL MOTHER	4¾″	P	340	255	160	125	120
68/2/0	LOST SHEEP	4¼″	P	180	135	85	65	65
/0		5½″	P	240	180	110	90	85
69	HAPPY PASTIME	3½″	P	240	180	160	140	100
III/69 CBX	Happy Pastime	6″	P	340	255	160	125	90
70	HOLY CHILD	6¾″	P	240	180	110	90	70
71	STORMY WEATHER	6¼″	P	800	600	370	290	230
72	SPRING CHEER	5″	P	300*	200*	100*	65	60
	*for yellow dress, no flower							
73	LITTLE HELPER	4¼″	P	180	135	85	65	80
74	LITTLE GARDENER	4″	P	180	135	85	65	60
	Dark green pants rare in TMK-1.							
75 HWF	Angelic Prayer	1¾″ × 3½″	P	70	50	32	25	20
76/A&B BE	Doll Mother & Prayer Before Battle	UNK	D	?	?	?	?	NA
77	(UNKNOWN)	?	C					
78/0/II	INFANT OF KRUMBAD	2″	D	?	?	?	?	NA
/I/II		2½″	P	–	–	37	30	20
/II/11		3½″	P	–	–	55	45	25
/III/11		4½″	P	–	120	75	60	30
/V/11		7¾″	D?	?	?	?	?	NA
/VIII/11		13½″	D?	?	?	?	?	NA
	Rare. If found w/old mark, mid 4-digit.							
/I/83		2½″	R					15
/II/83		3½″	R					20
/III/83		4¼″	R					30
/IV/83		–	?					NA
/V/83		7¾″	R					75
/VI/83		10″	R	500	400	?	?	175
/VIII/83		13½″	R	700	600			225
79	GLOBE TROTTER	5″	P	240	180	110	90	90
80	LITTLE SCHOLAR	5½″	P	240	180	110	90	80
81/2/0	SCHOOL GIRL	4¼″	P	180	135	85	65	75
/0		5″	P	240	200	110	90	110
	Delete 81/II from HUM. ART.							
82/2/0	SCHOOL BOY	4″	P	180	135	85	65	65
/0		5″	P	240	180	110	90	80
/II		7¾″	R	2,000	1,500	900	?	250

Number/ Size Mark	Name	Size	Status	TMK-1 Crown	TMK-2 Full Bee	TMK-3 Styl. Bee	TMK-4 3/Line	TMK-5 V/Gee
83	ANGEL SERENADE	5½″	R	650	500	400	?	200
84/0	WORSHIP	5″	P	280	210	130	100	90
	May be found as 84.—add 20%.							
/II		?	D	?	?	?	?	NA
/III		?	D	?	?	?	?	NA
/IV		?	D	?	?	?	?	NA
/V		12¾″	P	2500	1,800	1,200	?	900
85/0	SERENADE	4¾″	P	200	150	90	70	65
/I		?	D?					
/II		7½″	R	–	550	350	275	200
	May be found as 84/2—add 30%.							
86	HAPPINESS	4¾″	P	190	135	75	65	60
87	FOR FATHER	5½″	P	240	180	110	90	85
88/0	HEAVENLY PROTECTION	9″	D	?	?	?	?	NA
	Add to HUM. ART, p.123, low 4-digit.							
/I		6¾″	P	560	420	260	200	180
/II		9″	P	750	600	420	325	250
	HUM. ART, p.123, delete ref. to Table III.							
89/I	LITTLE CELLIST	6″	P	240	180	110	90	85
/II		7½″	P	–	–	350	275	220
90/A&B	Wayside Devotion & Adoration	?	D	?	?	?	?	NA
BE	*See HUM. ART, p.95.*							
91/A&B	Angels at Prayer	2″ × 4¾″	P	140	100	65	50	40
HWF	*(2 pcs.—left and right. Prices are per pr.)*							
92	Merry Wanderer	4¾″ × 5″	P	280	210	130	100	80
PLQ	*Reported in & out of production.*							
93	Little Fiddler	5″ × 5½″	R	300	200	150	?	80
PLQ								
94/3/0	SURPRISE	4″	P	200	150	100	80	70
/0		5″	D	400	350	300	?	NA
	Reported w/94. over 82, mid 4-digit price.							
/I		5½″	P	300	225	150	115	95
95	BROTHER	4¾″	P	200	150	90	70	60
96	LITTLE SHOPPER	5½″	P	180	135	85	65	60
97	TRUMPET BOY	4¾″	P	180	135	85	65	60
98/2/0	SISTER	4¾″	P	180	135	85	65	60
/0		5½″	P	200	150	90	70	70
99	EVENTIDE	4¾″ × 4¼″	P	400	300	185	145	120
100	Shrine	7½″	D	*	–	–	–	NA
TLP	**See HUM. ART, p.111 if found.*							
101	To Market	?	D	?	*	–	–	NA
TLP	*Reported w/TMK-3. *Low 4-digit figure.*							
102	Volunteers	?	D/R					NA
TLP	*None known. Est. price if found—low 4-digit. May be reissued 1979 or later.*							
103	Farewell	?	D					NA
TLP	*None known. Est. price if found—low 4-digit.*							
104	Wayside Devotion	?	D					NA
TLP	*None known. Est. price if found—low 4-digit.*							
105	ADORATION WITH BIRD	5½″	?	*				NA
	**See HUM. ART, p.107, for complete story.*							
106	Merry Wanderer	?	D?					NA
PLQ	*Example reported found in 1978. See HUM. ART, p.111 for complete story.*							
107	Little Fiddler	6″ × 5½″	D?					NA
PLQ	*Example found in 1978. See illus. p. 18. High 4-digit figure.*							
108	(UNKNOWN)	?	C					

Number/ Size Mark	Name	Size	Status	TMK-1 Crown	TMK-2 Full Bee	TMK-3 Styl. Bee	TMK-4 3/Line	TMK-5 V/Gee
109/0	HAPPY TRAVELLER	5″	P	190	140	95	70	65
/I		?	D?					
	Est. price if found—low 4-digit.							
/II		7½″	P	?	?	350	275	220
110/0	LET'S SING	3″	R	300	250	175	120	100
	Note: Size is 3″, not 3¼″.							
/I		4″	P	?	?	?	?	125
	Copyright date should read 1938.							
III/110 CBX	Let's Sing	6″	P	?	?	160	125	95
111/3/0	WAYSIDE HARMONY	4″	P	180	135	85	65	65
/2/0		?	D?					
/I		5″	P	300	225	140	110	90
	Correct copyright date is 1938.							
112/3/0	JUST RESTING	4″	P	180	135	85	65	65
/2/0		?	D?					
/I		5″	P	300	225	140	110	90
	Correct copyright date is 1938.							
113	HEAVENLY SONG	3½″ × 4¾″	R	?	?	?	?	125
	See HUM. ART, p.109 for information.							
114 AT	Let's Sing	3½″ × 6¼″	P	?	?	130	100	80
115-6-7 CAN	Christmas Angels	3½″	P	?	?	?	?	90
	Priced as set of 3.							
118	LITTLE THRIFTY	5″	P	300	225	140	110	110
119	POSTMAN	5″	P	280	210	130	100	120
120	JOYFUL, LET'S SING	?	D	?	?	?	?	NA
	No example known. If found, low 4-digit.							
121	WAYSIDE HARMONY— JUST RESTING	?	D	?	?	?	?	NA
	No example known. If found, low 4-digit.							
122	PUPPY LOVE— SERENADE HAPPINESS	?	D	?	?	?	?	NA
	No example known. If found, low 4-digit.							
123	MAX AND MORITZ	5″	P	250	210	130	100	90
124	HELLO		D	?	?	?	?	NA
/0		6¼″	P	185	150	90	75	75
/I		7″	R	500±	300	?	?	150
	See HUM. ART, p.124 for details.							
125 PLQ	Vacation Time	4″ × 4¾″	P	360	270	165	130	110
	See HUM. ART, p.112 for details.							
126 PLQ	Retreat to Safety	4¾″ × 4¾″	R	250	180	125	100	100
	Reinstated in U.S. catalog, May 1, 1978.							
127	DOCTOR	4¾″	P	240	180	110	90	75
	Design variations exist—add 30%.							
128	BAKER	4¾″	P	250	180	110	90	75
129	BAND LEADER	5″	P	280	210	130	100	80
130	DUET	5″	P	350	25	165	130	110
131	STREET SINGER	5″	P	200	150	90	70	70
132	STAR GAZER	4¾″	P	280	210	130	100	85
133	MOTHER'S HELPER	5″	P	280	210	130	100	85
134 PLQ	Quartet	6″ × 6″	P	–	250	200	175	150
135	SOLOIST	4¾″	P	175	135	85	65	65

Number/Size Mark	Name	Size	Status	TMK-1 Crown	TMK-2 Full Bee	TMK-3 Styl. Bee	TMK-4 3/Line	TMK-5 V/Gee
136/I	FRIENDS	5"	P	?	210	130	100	90
/V		10¾"	P	*	*	*	600	550
/5		11½"	D	1,500	1,200	900	–	
	See HUM. ART, p.108 for details.							
137 PLQ	Child in Bed	2¾" × 2¾"	P	160	120	75	60	40
138	(UNKNOWN)	?	C					
139 PLQ	Flitting Butterfly	2½" × 2½"	R	375	240	200	?	75
	Also called "Sitting Child with Butterfly." *Not in all U.S. catalogs.*							
140 PLQ	Mail Coach	6¼" × 4¼"	P	400	280	200	160	145
141/3/0	APPLE TREE GIRL	4"	P	200	135	85	65	65
	No bird in tree in this size.							
/2/0		?	D?					
/0		?	D?	?	?	?	?	NA
/I		6"	P	350	250	165	130	120
/V		10"	P	–	–	?	500±	550
/X		29"	P	–	–	–	–	11,800
	141/II, 141/III, 141/IV omitted. No known examples.							
142/3/0	APPLE TREE BOY	4"	P	200	135	85	65	65
/I		6"	P	350	250	165	130	120
/V		10"	P				550	550
/X		29"	P					11,800
	142/II, 142/III, 142/IV omitted. No known examples.							
143/0	BOOTS	5½"	P	240	180	110	90	75
/I		6½"	R	800	600	450	250	200
144	ANGELIC SONG	4"	P	225	160	110	90	80
	Blue flowers in headband are standard.							
145	LITTLE GUARDIAN	4"	P	225	160	110	90	75
	Premium w/blue flowers in headband—25%.							
146 HWF	Angel Duet	3¼" × 4¾"	P	90	70	45	35	25
147 HWF	Devotion	3" × 5"	P	90	70	45	35	25
148	(UNKNOWN)	?	C					
149	(UNKNOWN)	?	C					
150/2/0	HAPPY DAYS	4¼"	P	300	225	140	100	95
/0		5¼"	R	?	450	300	?	175
/I		6¼"	R	1,200	900	600	?	275
	Correct size is 6¼", not 6½" in HUM. ART.							
151/W	MADONNA, SEATED & CHILD (White)	12"	R	*	*	–	–	400
/II	MADONNA, SEATED & CHILD (Blue)	12"	R	*	*	–	–	800
	When found, est. price low 4-digit. With brown cloak, 5-digit.							
152A	UMBRELLA BOY	?	D?					
	May be on Plate in early '80s.							
/0		4¾"	P	?	600	450	350	300
/I		?	D	?	?	?	?	
/II		8"	P	?	1,200	850	750	700
152B	UMBRELLA GIRL	?	D?					
	May be on Plate in early '80s.							
/0		4¾"	P		600	450	350	300
/I		?	D?					
/II		8"	P		1,200	850	750	700

Number/ Size Mark	Name	Size	Status	TMK-1 Crown	TMK-2 Full Bee	TMK-3 Styl. Bee	TMK-4 3/Line	TMK-5 V/Gee
153	AUF WIEDERSEHEN	6¾"	D?					
/0		5"	P	320	240	150	115	120
/I		7"	R	400	300	200		225
	Rare example found w/hat—low 4-digit price.							
154	WAITER	6½"	D?					
	May be reissued in 1979 or later.							
/0		6"	P	280	210	130	100	85
/I		7"	R	–	750	600	–	200
155-162	(UNKNOWN)	?	C					
	No examples reported to date.							
163	WHITSUNTIDE	7"	R	1,800	1,500	1,200	?	450
	See HUM. ART, p.113 for additional info.							
164 HWF	Worship	2¾" × 4¾"	P	?	65	45	35	25
165 PLQ	Swaying Lullaby	5¼" × 5¼"	R	2,000	1,500	1,200	?	200
166 AT	Boy with Bird	3¼" × 6¼"	P	300	225	140	100	80
167 HWF	Angel w/Yellow Bird	3" × 4¾"	R	100	85	65	50	50
	Reinstated in U.S. catalog May 1, 1978.							
168 PLQ	Standing Boy	5¾" × 5¾"	R	2,000	1,500	1,200	?	200
169	BIRD DUET	4"	P	240	180	110	90	75
170/0	SCHOOLBOYS	?	D?					
/I		7½"	P			900	725	500
/II		?	D?					
/III		10¼"	P	**	**	*	*	1,200
	***Mid 4-digit. *Low 4-digit.*							
171	LITTLE SWEEPER	4¼"	P	180	135	85	65	60
172/0	FESTIVAL HARMONY W/MANDOLIN	8"	P	?	350	200	165	140
/I		?	D?					
/II		10¼"	P	1,500	*	420	325	240
	No examples reported—$1,000 est. value.							
173/0	FESTIVAL HARMONY W/FLUTE	8"	P	?	350	200	165	140
/I		?	D?					
/II		10¼"	P	1,500	*	420	325	240
	No examples reported—$1,000 est. value.							
174	SHE LOVES ME, SHE LOVES ME NOT	4¼"	P	250	175	130	100	80
	Old marks have eyes open.							
175	MOTHER'S DARLING	5½"	P	250	175	130	100	85
176/0	HAPPY BIRTHDAY	5½"	P	320	240	150	120	95
	See HUM. ART, p.127 for more info.							
/I		6"	R	*	?	?	?	250
	TMK-1 w/decimal reported ($600).							
177/0	SCHOOL GIRLS	?	D?					
/I		7½"	P	–	–	750	600	500
/II		?	D?					
/III		9½"	P	–	–	1,500	1,200	1,200
178	THE PHOTOGRAPHER	5¼"	P	–	250	160	125	130
	Copyright date reported as 1948.							
179	COQUETTES	5"	P	320	250	160	125	110
180 PLQ	Tuneful Good Night	5" x 4¾"	R	900	750	650	?	200

Number/ Size Mark	Name	Size	Status	TMK-1 Crown	TMK-2 Full Bee	TMK-3 Styl. Bee	TMK-4 3/Line	TMK-5 V/Gee
181	MAMAS AND PAPAS	8″	D	?	?	?	?	
	One of a set of four known. Very rare. 5-digit figure, each.							
182	GOOD FRIENDS	4″	P	?	175	120	95	85
183	FOREST SHRINE	9″	R	2,000	1,500	1,200	850	550
184	LATEST NEWS	5″	P	360	270	165	130	110
	See HUM. ART, p.110 for details.							
185	ACCORDION BOY	5″	P	210	160	110	90	75
186	SWEET MUSIC	5″	P	225	175	120	95	80
187 PLQ	Hummel Display Plaque	4″ × 5½″	D	*	*	*		
	*See HUM. ART, p.109 for details.							
187C		5½″ × 3-5/8″	P	–	–	–	?	50
	Note: Redesigned English Display Plaque. Late '60s or early '70s.							
188	CELESTIAL MUSICIAN	7″	P	425	350	225	175	125
189	MAMAS AND PAPAS	8″	D	?	?	?	?	NA
	One of a set of four known. 5-digit figure, each.							
190	MAMAS AND PAPAS	8″	D	?	?	?	?	NA
	One of a set of four known. 5-digit figure, each.							
191	MAMAS AND PAPAS	8″	D	?	?	?	?	NA
	One of a set of four known. 5-digit figure, each.							
192 CAN	Candlelight	6¾″	R	?	500	400	–	125
	See HUM. ART, p.108 for variations & est. prices.							
193 CAN	Angel Duet	5″	P	–	–	–	120	95
	See HUM. ART, p.81 for info. Reinstated May '78.							
194 CAN	Angelic Care	6½″	P	360	270	165	130	160
	Note: Known as WATCHFUL ANGEL & GUARDIAN ANGEL.							
195/2/0	BARNYARD HERO	4″	P	240	180	110	90	75
/0		?	D?					
/I		5½″	P	400	300	185	145	125
196/2/0	TELLING HER SECRET	?	D/R					
	Reissue expected in 1979 or later.							
/0		5″	P	–	300	185	145	135
	Reported w/TMK-3 w. 192., price about $250.							
/I		6½″	R	–	600	450	?	300
197/2/0	BE PATIENT	4¼″	P	?	180	110	90	75
/0		?	D?					
/I		6¼″	P	?	260	160	125	110
	Copyright date reported as 1948.							
198/2/0	HOME FROM MARKET	4¾″	P	200	150	90	70	65
	See HUM. ART, p.109 for details & price.							
/0		?	D?					
–		?	D?	?	300±	–	–	NA
	Produced as only 198 & 198. in 1950s.							
/I		5½″	P	280	210	130	100	85
	See HUM. ART, p.109 for variation & price.							
199	FEEDING TIME	5½″	D?	600	400	?	?	NA
	Reported w/dec. point. Price about $400±.							
/0		4¼″	P	250	200	120	95	85
/I		5½″	P	*	240	150	120	95
	Reported w/dbl. crown. Est. $600±.							
200	LITTLE GOAT HERDER	5¾″	D	?	300	–	–	NA
	Found w/dec. point. Approx. price w/crown TMK-1 $500±.							
/0		4¾″	P		180	110	90	80
/I		5½″	P	?	240	150	120	90
	See HUM. ART, pp.89,100 for details.							

Number/ Size Mark	Name	Size	Status	TMK-1 Crown	TMK-2 Full Bee	TMK-3 Styl. Bee	TMK-4 3/Line	TMK-5 V/Gee
201/2/0	RETREAT TO SAFETY	4″	P	?	150	90	70	75
/0		?	D?					
/I		5½″	P	350	250	175	140	120
	Found oversize. Add 30% to above prices.							
202	(UNKNOWN)	?	C					
203/2/0	SIGNS OF SPRING	4″	P	240	180	110	90	75
	Note: Design variation with shoes on both feet worth $400-$500.							
/0		?	D?					NA
/I		5½″	P	300	225	140	110	95
204	WEARY WANDERER	6″	P	260	200	120	95	90
205 PLQ	HUMMEL DISPLAY Plaque	4″ × 5½″	D	?	?	?	?	NA
	Refer to HUM. ART, p.88 for more and p.109 for prices.							
206 HWF	Angel Cloud	2¼″ × 4¾″	R	400	350	300	250	100
	Reinstated in U.S. catalog, May 1, 1978.							
207 HWF	Heavenly Angel	2″ × 4¾″	P	90	70	43	33	25
208 PLQ	HUMMEL DISPLAY Plaque	4″ × 5½″	D	?	?	?	?	NA
	See HUM. ART, p.88 and p.109 for details & price.							
209 PLQ	HUMMEL DISPLAY Plaque	4″ × 5½″	D	?	?	?	?	NA
	See HUM. ART, p.88 & p.109 for details & price.							
210 PLQ	HUMMEL DISPLAY Plaque	4″ × 5½″	D	?	?	?	?	NA
	This plaque has "Schmid Bros" on bag. Est. price low 4-digit figure.							
211 PLQ	HUMMEL DISPLAY Plaque	4″ × 5½″	D	?	?	?	?	NA
	All white plaque reported in this design.							
212 PLQ	HUMMEL DISPLAY Plaque	4″ × 5½″	D	?	?	?	?	NA
	HUM. ART, p.128 should read 210.							
213 PLQ	HUMMEL DISPLAY Plaque	4″ × 5½″	D	?	?	?	?	NA
	Refer to HUM. ART, p.88 & p.128 for details and prices.							
214 NAT Sml.	*NATIVITY SET (12 pieces)		P	–	?	?	750	675
	Twelve-piece set w/TMK-2 in white at $1,500.							
214 NAT Sml.	*NATIVITY SET (16 pieces)		P	–	?	?	900	775
	For prices of individual pieces refer to HUM. ART, p. 129 and add 50% for CMP.							
215	(UNKNOWN)	?	C					
216	(UNKNOWN)	?	C					
217	BOY WITH TOOTHACHE	5½″	P	?	175	120	95	75
	Copyright 1951.							
218/2/0	BIRTHDAY SERENADE	4¼″	P	?	200	150	95	80
	See HUM. ART, p.107 for variations & price.							
/0		5¼″	R	?	350	225	150	175
	See HUM. ART, p.108 for variations & price.							
219/2/0	LITTLE VELMA (correct name)	4″	D?					
	Very rare. See HUM. ART, p.108 (GIRL W/FROG) for story & prices.							
220	WE CONGRATULATE	4″	P	?	150	100	80	75
	See HUM. ART, p.95 for more information.							
221	(UNKNOWN)	?	C					
222 PLQ	Madonna	4″ × 5″	D?					
	See HUM. ART, p.90 for details and prices.							
M223 TLP	To Market	9½″	P	–	500	370	285	200
M224/I TLP	Wayside Harmony	7½″	P	–	?	286	224	180
/II		9½″	R	?	*	?	?	220
	See HUM. ART, p.113 for price of old marks.							

Number/ Size Mark	Name	Size	Status	TMK-1 Crown	TMK-2 Full Bee	TMK-3 Styl. Bee	TMK-4 3/Line	TMK-5 V/Gee
M225/I TLP	Just Resting	7½″	P	–	450	286	224	175
/II		9½″	R	?	*	?	?	220
	Example of TMK-2 reported at $500.							
226	MAIL IS HERE	6″ × 4¼″	P	–	700	500	400	275
M227 TLP	She Loves Me/She Loves Me Not	7½″	P	–	?	275	225	175
M228 TLP	Good Friends	7½″	P	700	450	275	225	175
M229 TLP	Apple Tree Girl	7½″	P	–	450	275	225	175
M230 TLP	Apple Tree Boy	7½″	P	–	450	275	225	175
M231 TLP	Birthday Serenade	9¾″	R	?	?	?	?	240
	See HUM. ART, p.129 for more information.							
M232 TLP	Happy Days	9¾″	R	?	?	?	?	240
	See HUM. ART, p.128 for rarity and price.							
233	(UNKNOWN)	?	C					
M234 TLP	Birthday Serenade	7½″	R	?	?	?	?	220
M235 TLP	Happy Days	7½″	R	?	?	?	?	220
236	(UNKNOWN)	?	C					
237	(UNKNOWN)	?	C					
238/A	ANGEL TRIO (B) w/Banjo	2½″	P	–	175	100	75	75
/B	ANGEL TRIO (B) w/Accordion	2″	P	–	175	100	75	75
/C	ANGEL TRIO (B) w/Horn	2½″	P	–	175	100	75	75
	Same as CAN III38, III39, and III40 except for candleholders.							
239/A	CHILDREN TRIO (A)							
	Girl w/Flower	3½″	–	?	?	?	?	30
/B	CHILDREN TRIO (A)							
	Girl w/Doll	3½″	–	?	?	?	?	30
/C	CHILDREN TRIO (A)							
	Boy w/Horse	3½″	–	?	?	?	?	30
	Price is for set of three (A, B, and C).							
240	DRUMMER	4¼″	P	?	150	90	70	60
241 CAN	Angel Light (Angel Bridge)	8-3/8″	*	–	–	–	–	200
	HUM. ART lists as unk. Issued in 1978, cataloged in U.S. in 1979. First called Angel Bridge.							
242	(UNKNOWN)	?	C					
243 HWF	Madonna and Child	3″ × 4″	R	?	?	?	?	25
244	(UNKNOWN)	?	C					
245	(UNKNOWN)	?	C					
246 HWF	Holy Family	3½″ × 4″	P	–	75	45	35	30
247	(UNKNOWN)	?	C					
248 HWF	Kneeling Angel	2¼″ × 5½″	P	–	65	40	30	25
249	(UNKNOWN)	?	C					
250/A&B BE	Little Goatherder							
	& Feeding Time	5½″	P	–	350	225	175	150
	Above prices are for the pr.							
251/A&B BE	Good Friends & She Loves							
	Me/She Loves Me Not	5″	P	–		225	175	150
	Above prices are for the pr.							

Number/Size Mark	Name	Size	Status	TMK-1 Crown	TMK-2 Full Bee	TMK-3 Styl. Bee	TMK-4 3/Line	TMK-5 V/Gee
252/A&B BE	Apple Tree Girl & Apple Tree Boy	5″	P	–	300	185	145	130
	Above prices are for the pr.							
253	(UNKNOWN)	?	C					
254	(UNKNOWN)	?	C					
255	STITCH IN TIME	6¾″	P	?	?	?	100	95
256	KNITTING LESSON	7½″	P	–	–	–	275	220
257	FOR MOTHER	5″	P	–	–	90	70	65
	Note: Copyright 1963.							
258	WHICH HAND?	5½″	P	–	150	90	70	65
259	(UNKNOWN)	?	C					
260 NAT Lrg.	*NATIVITY SET (16 pieces)		P	–	–	–	2,500	2,250
	For prices of individual pieces refer to HUM. ART, p.131 and add 50% for CMP.							
261	ANGEL DUET	5″	P	–	–	200	130	100
	Delete comment HUM. ART, p.81.							
262	HEAVENLY LULLABY	3½″ × 5″	P	–	–	100	80	80
	Illus. 114, p.49, HUM. ART should be titled HEAVENLY LULLABY.							
263 PLQ	Merry Wanderer	4¾″ × 5″	D	?	?	?	?	NA
	HUM. ART, p. 111 for information & price, if found.							
264	ANNUAL PLATE 1971 [1]	7½″	D	–	–	–	1	1,000
	Heavenly Angel, known with TMK-4, add 30%. Other variations known.							
265	ANNUAL PLATE 1972	7½″	D	–	–	–	–	100
	Hear Ye, Hear Ye							
266	ANNUAL PLATE 1973	7½″	D	–	–	–	–	220
	Globetrotter							
267	ANNUAL PLATE 1974	7½″	D	–	–	–	–	120
	Goose Girl							
268	ANNUAL PLATE 1975	7½″	D	–	–	–	–	100
	Ride into Christmas							
269	ANNUAL PLATE 1976	7½″	D	–	–	–	–	100
	Apple Tree Girl							
270	ANNUAL PLATE 1977	7½″	D	–	–	–	–	150
	Apple Tree Boy							
271	ANNUAL PLATE 1978	7½″	D	–	–	–	–	150
	Happy Pastime							
272	ANNUAL PLATE 1979	7½″	D	–	–	–	–	125
	SINGING LESSON [1] *May vary throughout issue year within broad limits.*							
	Original issue price in year indicated.							
273	ANNUAL PLATE 1980	7½″	A					
	Reported this may be "School Girl"?							
274	ANNUAL PLATE 1981	7½″	A					
	Reported this may be "Umbrella Boy"?							
275	ANNUAL PLATE 1982	7½″	A					
	Reported this may be "Umbrella Girl"?							
276	ANNUAL PLATE 1983	7½″	A					
	Reported this may be "Postman"?							
277	ANNUAL PLATE 1984	7½″	A					
	Reported this may be "Autumn Harvest"?							
278	ANNUAL PLATE 1985	7½″	A					
	Reported this may be "Chick Girl"?							
279	ANNUAL PLATE 1986	7½″	A					
	Reported this may be "Playmates"?							
280	ANNIVERSARY PLATE 1975		D					350
	Stormy Weather							
281-299	OPEN (for assignment to subject at some future date)							

Number/Size Mark	Name	Size	Status	TMK-1 Crown	TMK-2 Full Bee	TMK-3 Styl. Bee	TMK-4 3/Line	TMK-5 V/Gee
300	TENDERNESS	UNK	P	–	–	–	–	200
	A new figurine being introduced in 1979 which was copyrighted in 1956.							
301	DELIVERY ANGEL W/BASKETS		A	–	*	?	?	NA
	Expect release in 1979. Reported w/TMK-2. If found, low 4-digit figure.							
302	KNIT ONE, PURL ONE		A	–	–	–	–	NA
	Presumed name. Official name when issued in 1979 or later may be different.							
303	SCHOOL LESSON		A	–	–	–	–	NA
	Presumed name. Official name when issued in 1979 or later may be different.							
304	ARTIST	5½"	P	–	?	?	100	85
305	BUILDER	5½"	P	–	?	150	110	90
306	LITTLE BOOKKEEPER	4¾"	P	–	–	?	140	120
307	GOOD HUNTING	5"	P	–	?	?	110	90
	Possible design variation reported w/TMK-4.							
308	LITTLE TAILOR	5½"	P	–	?	165	130	110
309	GREETINGS		A	–	–	–	–	
	Presumed name. Official name when issued in 1979 or later may be different.							
310/A	SEARCHING ANGEL	4-1/8" × 3-3/8"	P	–	–	–	–	80
	New introduction. First listed in Jan. 1979 catalog.							
311	KISS ME	6"	P	–	–	150	110	90
	Expect figure w/o socks only in TMK-3. No examples in #1 or #2 marks.							
312	JAM POT		A	–	–	–	–	NA
	Presumed name. Official name when issued in 1979 or later may differ.							
313	ASSIGNED		A	–	–	–	–	NA
	Number allocated for future design & copyright.							
314	CONFIDENTIALLY	5½"	P	–	1,000	?	120	90
	Older models have no bowtie. See HUM. ART, pp. 108 and 132.							
315	MOUNTAINEER	5"	P	–	?	150	110	90
316	ASSIGNED		A	–	–	–	–	NA
	Number allocated for future design & copyright.							
317	NOT FOR YOU	6"	P	–	–	150	110	90
318	ASSIGNED		A	–	–	–	–	NA
	Number allocated for future design & copyright.							
319	DOLL BATH	5"	P	–	–	150	110	80
	Copyright 1956—released in 1962.							
320	PROFESSOR	6"	A	–	–	–	–	NA
	Presumed name. Official name when issued in 1979 or later may differ.							
321	WASH DAY	6"	P	–	–	140	110	90
	Copyright 1956—probably released in '60s.							
322	LITTLE PHARMACIST	6"	P	–	–	?	110	90
	Copyright 1957—probably issued in 1960s.							
323 PLQ	MERRY CHRISTMAS	5-1/8"	P	–	–	–		110
	New introduction. First listed in Jan. 1979 catalog.							
324	OTHER SIDE OF THE FENCE		A	–	–	–	–	NA
	Presumed name. Official name when issued in 1979 or later may vary.							
325	MOTHER'S AID		A	–	–	–	–	NA
	Expect initial release in 1979.							
326	NAUGHTY BOY		A	–	–	–	–	NA
	Expect initial release in 1979.							
327	RUNAWAY (THE)	5½"	P	–	–	*	125	120
	See HUM. ART, p.112 for details on design changes. If found $250.							
328	CARNIVAL	6"	P	–	–	?	90	75
	Copyright date 1956. Issue date 1963(?).							
329	KINDERGARTEN ROMANCE		A	–	–	–	–	NA
	Presumed name. Official name when issued in 1979 or later may vary.							
330	KNEADING DOUGH		A	–	–	–	–	NA
	Presumed name. Official name when issued in 1979 or later may vary.							

Number/ Size Mark	Name	Size	Status	TMK-1 Crown	TMK-2 Full Bee	TMK-3 Styl. Bee	TMK-4 3/Line	TMK-5 V/Gee
331	CROSSROADS	6¾"	P	–	–	250	200	200
	Copyright 1956. Issue date 1972.							
332	SOLDIER BOY	6"	P	–	–	90	70	75
	Copyright date 1956. Issue date 1963±.							
333	BLESSED EVENT	5½"	P	–	?	275	220	200
	Copyright date 1956. Issue date 1971.							
334	HOMEWARD BOUND	5¼"	P	–	–	?	220	175
	Copyright date 1956. Issue date 1971.							
335	ASSIGNED		A	–	–	–	–	NA
	Number allocated for future design and copyright.							
336	CLOSE HARMONY	5½"	P	–	–	–	125	120
	Note: Hair on short girl may vary.							
337	CINDERELLA	4½"	P	–	–	–	125	120
	Rare example with eyes open known.							
338	BIRTHDAY WISH, A		A	–	–	–	–	NA
	Expected initial release in 1979.							
339	WALKING HER DOG		A	–	–	–	–	NA
	Assumed name. Official name when issued in 1979 or later may vary.							
340	LETTER TO SANTA CLAUS	7¼"	P	–	–	–	190	165
341	BIRTHDAY PRESENT		A	–	–	–	–	
	Assumed name. Official name when issued in 1979 or later may vary.							
342	MISCHIEF MAKER	5"	P	–	–	180	140	120
343	SINGING ANGEL		A	–	–	–	–	NA
	Presumed name. Official name when issued in 1979 or later may vary.							
344	FEATHERED FRIENDS	4¾"	P	–	–	–	140	115
345	A FAIR MEASURE	5½"	P	–	–	–	140	115
346	SMART LITTLE SISTER	4¾"	P	–	–	150	115	95
	Copyright 1956. Issued date c.1962.							
347	ADVENTURE BOUND	8¼" × 7½"	P	–	2,800*	?	?	1,650
	TMK-2 reported. Existence of TMK-3 doubtful.							
348	RING AROUND THE ROSIE	6¾"	P	–	–	2,000	1,750	1,500
	In 1969 price list this piece was $100.							
349	FLOWER LOVER		A	–	–	–	–	NA
	Presumed name. Official name when issued in 1979 or later may vary.							
350	HOLIDAY SHOPPER		A	–	–	–	–	NA
	Presumed name. Official name when issued in 1979 or later may vary.							
351	REMEMBERING		A	–	–	–	–	NA
	Presumed name. Official name when issued in 1979 or later may vary.							
352	MUSICAL GOOD MORNING		A	–	–	–	–	NA
	Presumed name. Official name when issued in 1979 or later may vary.							
353	SPRING DANCE	?	D?	–	–	–	?	NA
	*No examples reported w/number 353 **only**.*							
/0		5¼"	R	–	–	?	350	400
	Copyright 1963. Probable issue, 1964. Reissued in Canada in 1978. See Table B.							
/I		6¼"	P	–	–	475	360	300
	Copyright 1977. Probable issue, 1964.							
354	ASSIGNED		A	–	–	–	–	NA
	Number allocated for future design & copyright.							
355	AUTUMN HARVEST	4¾"	P	–	–	–	115	90
	Copyright 1964.							
356	GAY ADVENTURE	5"	P	–	–	–	115	85
	Copyright 1971. Issue date 1972.							
357	GUIDING ANGEL	2¾"	P	–	–	75	60	40
	Copyright 1961. Issue date uncertain.							
358	SHINING LIGHT	2¾"	P	–	–	75	60	40
	Copyright 1961. Issue date uncertain.							

Number/Size Mark	Name	Size	Status	TMK-1 Crown	TMK-2 Full Bee	TMK-3 Styl. Bee	TMK-4 3/Line	TMK-5 V/Gee
359	TUNEFUL ANGEL	2¾″	P	–	–	75	60	45
	Copyright date 1956. Issue date uncertain.							
360/A WVS	Boy & Girl	6¼″	R	–	–	?	?	100
	Copyright 1958. Date of original issue unknown. Relisted in 1979.							
/B	Boy	6¼″	R	–	–	?	?	100
	Copyright 1958. Date of original issue unknown. Relisted in 1979.							
/C	Girl	6¼″	R	–	–	?	?	100
	Copyright 1958. Date of original issue unknown. Relisted in 1979.							
361	FAVORITE PET	4¼″	P	–	–	–	115	95
	Copyright 1961. Issue date about 1966(?).							
362	THOUGHTFUL		A	–	–	–	–	NA
	Presumed name. Official name may differ when issued in 1979 or later.							
363	BIG HOUSECLEANING	4″	P	–	–	–	–	120
	Copyright 1961. Issue date probably late '60s.							
364	MADONNA AND CHILD		A	–	–	–	–	NA
	New issue expected in 1979 or later.							
365	WEE ANGEL		A	–	–	–	–	NA
	New issue expected in 1979 or later.							
366	FLYING ANGEL	3½″	P	–	–	75	60	60
	Copyright 1964. Release date uncertain.							
/W		3½″	P	–	–	28	22	18
367	BUSY STUDENT	4½″	P	–	–	110	90	75
	Copyright 1967. Release date uncertain.							
368	ASSIGNED		A	–	–	–	–	NA
	Number allocated for future design.							
369	FOLLOW THE LEADER	7″	P	–	–	–	600	435
	Copyright date 1967. Release date uncertain.							
370-373	ASSIGNED		A	–	–	–	–	NA
	Numbers allocated for future designs.							
374	LOST STOCKING	4½″	P	–	–	120	95	75
	Copyright date 1965. Release date unknown.							
375-376	ASSIGNED		A	–	–	–	–	NA
	Numbers allocated for future designs.							
377	BASHFUL	4¾″	P	–	–	–	95	80
	Copyright date 1971. Release early '70s.							
378	EASTER GREETINGS	5¼″	P	–	–	–	115	85
	Copyright date 1971. Release date early '70s.							
379-380	ASSIGNED		A	–	–	–	–	NA
	Numbers allocated for future designs.							
381	FLOWER VENDOR	5¼″	P	–	–	–	115	85
	Copyright date 1971. Release date early '70s.							
382	VISITING AN INVALID	5″	P	–	–	–	145	115
	Copyright date 1971. Release date early '70s.							
383	ASSIGNED		A	–	–	–	–	NA
	Number allocated for future design.							
384	EASTER TIME	4″	P	–	–	–	135	115
	Copyright date 1971.							
385	CHICKEN-LICKEN	4¾″	P	–	–	–	145	115
	Copyright date 1971. Release date in '70s.							
386	ON SECRET PATH	5¼″	P	–	–	–	135	125
	Copyright date 1971. Release date in '70s.							
387	VALENTINE GIFT	5-5/8″	D	–	–	–	–	300
	Size changed to 5-5/8″. *Special for 1978 Goebel Collectors' Club members. Issued at $45.							
388 CAN	Little Band	4¾″	P	–	–	–	–	120
	First listed in U.S.A. Price List May 1, 1978. ©1968.							

Number/ Size Mark	Name	Size	Status	TMK-1 Crown	TMK-2 Full Bee	TMK-3 Styl. Bee	TMK-4 3/Line	TMK-5 V/Gee
388/M MBX	Little Band (w/candle)	4¾″ × 5″	P	–	–	–	–	185
389-391	CHILDREN TRIO (B)	2¼″	P	–	–	–	120	100
	Price is for set of three. © 1968.							
392	LITTLE BAND	4¾″ × 3″	P	–	–	–	?	125
392/M MBX	Little Band w/o candle	4¾″ × 5″	P	–	–	–	?	180
393	OPEN		O					
	Number open for preliminary assignment of design for future issue.							
394	ASSIGNED		A	–	–	–	–	NA
	Number allocated to a future design.							
395	ASSIGNED		A	–	–	–	–	NA
	Number allocated to a future design.							
396	RIDE INTO CHRISTMAS	5¾″	P	–	–	?	325	320
	Excessive demand and price due to coupling w/1975 Plate for display.							
397	OPEN		O					
	Number open for preliminary assignment of design for future issue.							
398	OPEN		O					
	Number open for preliminary assignment of design for future issue.							
399	OPEN		O					
	Number open for preliminary assignment of design for future issue.							
HU-2 BU	HUMMEL BUST	5¾″	D*	–	–	–	–	100
	*Available to Goebel Collectors' Club only. Was in 5/1/78 catalog @ $15.							
690 PLQ	Smiling Through	?						
	Plaque reserved for 1979 members of Goebel Collectors' Club only.							
700 BL	ANNUAL BELL (First Issue—1978) Let's Sing	6¼″	P					200
701 BL	ANNUAL BELL (Second Issue—1979) Farewell *design.*	6¼″						90

¹ May be subject to wide price variations in secondary market.

REISSUES SINCE *HUMMEL ART* — A PROBLEM?

A reissue is a reinstated figurine which had been removed from production and sale for a varying period of years. Rumors that flourished in 1977 of such reinstatements materialized during 1978. A composite list of reissued figurines since the publication of *Hummel Art* appears in Table B on page 55. This list and prices were derived from several sources in the United States, Germany, and Canada.

Although collectors were excited by the news of reissues, many of them expressed concern that the reissues would cause problems with the value of older examples once thought to be rare, if not unique. The potential of such reissues to cause chaos in the secondary market is a very real danger. Collectors called upon Goebel to institute some simple moves to protect the integrity of the older, previously issued models.

Very few reissues were exported to the United States. The Goebel Company explained that this was due to their inability to fill the high demand in this country. Therefore, most pieces were released in Germany and Canada where demand is usually a fraction of that in this country. A glance at the "Current Market Price" column under U.S.A. shows that this strategy was unsuccessful. Dealers, already buying in the German and Canadian retail markets because of inadequate allotments of regular figurines, were on hand to snatch up these desirable reissues and ship them to the U.S. The "Current Market Price" column dramatically shows what will happen when the "have nots" with desire have the "wherewithall." At press time apparently additional reissued items are being furnished directly to American dealers by Goebel. Thus, 1979 appears to be a year with many uncertainties as to availability and a fair price for reissues.

One seemingly easy way that the Goebel Company could insure the integrity of older models would be to incorporate minor design changes on reissued pieces. Such changes would not affect the esthetic value of the models but would distinguish the new from the old. For example the number and arrangement of the blossoms on the tree trunk of Forest Shrine, 183, could be altered. With adequate publicity, such small changes would help the collector identify the "vintage" pieces at a glance.

If the reissues all carried the current trademark (TMK-6) they could at least be identified as such even though otherwise identical to the older, original issues. Unfortunately one serious exception was reported in which Whitsuntide, 163, discontinued some years ago, was being sold in the retail trade as a "reissue" but bearing TMK-3 (1960-67) rather than the recent TMK-5 on the bottom. At the same time identical pieces were also being reported with the recent TMK-5 mark. Perhaps some TMK-3 pieces were found in the factory, left from a previous production lot, and sent along to complete a shipment. The confusion, disappointment, and financial loss to owners who had purchased examples of the very scarce TMK-3 for over a thousand dollars because there would never be any more with this mark has been very real as a result of this incident. All of this could have been prevented by simply stamping underglaze the words "Reissued in 1978."

A statement by the company as to their intentions regarding the quanitities which may be reissued in the future would help all collectors. If these once-rare examples become common collectibles at relatively modest prices, collectors will suffer not only financial loss but also a loss of interest in Hummel collecting.

TABLE B

REISSUE AVAILABILITY AND PRICES*

(With U.S. and German prices in U.S. dollars; Canadian prices in Canadian dollars.)

Number/ Size Mark	Name	Size	U.S.A. Low	U.S.A. High	CANADA Low	CANADA High	GERMANY Low	GERMANY High
2/III	LITTLE FIDDLER	12½"	NA	1,000	525	NA	325	975
3/III	BOOKWORM	9½"	NA	1,000	525	NA	325	975
7/III	MERRY WANDERER	11¾"	NA	1,000	525	NA	325	975
13/II	MEDITATION	7"	NA	400	NA	NA	92	395
13/V	MEDITATION	13¾"	600	1,050	525	NA	325	975
24/III	CAN Lullaby	8¼" × 5½"	NA	400	205	NA	128	325
27/III	JOYOUS NEWS	4¼" × 4¼"	80	250	69	70	42	225
45/I/6	MADONNA W/HALO	12"	45	50	NA	NA	25	30
46/III/6	MADONNA, PRAYING	16¾"	85	100	79	80	50	80
46/III/W	MADONNA, PRAYING	16¾"	60	60	NA	NA	36	NA
48/II	PLQ Madonna	4¾" × 6"	80	100	79	90	45	95
49/I	TO MARKET	6¼"	NA	250	185	NA	110	225
50/0	VOLUNTEERS	5½"	80	90	90	NA	58	175
50/I	VOLUNTEERS	6¼"	NA	250	185	200	110	225
51/I	VILLAGE BOY	7¼"	NA	200	89	100	55	175
52/I	GOING TO GRANDMA'S	6"	NA	200	NA	NA	110	225
78/I/83	INFANT OF KRUMBAD	2½"	NA	12	NA	NA	8	NA
78/II/83		3½"	NA	20	NA	NA	13	NA
78/III/83		4¼"	NA	30	NA	NA	17	NA
78/V/83		7"	NA	75	NA	NA	25	55
78/VI/83		11"	NA	175	NA	NA	52	125
78/VIII/83		14"	NA	225	NA	NA	105	225
82/II	SCHOOL BOY	7½"	NA	275	175	NA	95	225
83	ANGEL SERENADE	5½"	65	200	NA	NA	42	225
85/II	SERENADE	7½"	170	190	154	NA	85	155
93	PLQ Little Fiddler	5" × 5½"	NA	60	46	50	29	55
110/0	LET'S SING	3"	45	80	NA	NA	28	75
113	HEAVENLY SONG	3½"	NA	125	NA	NA	48	113
124/I	HELLO	7"	NA	125	95	110	53	145
126	PLQ Retreat to Safety	4¾" × 4¾"	80	100	NA	NA	43	65
139	PLQ Flitting Butterfly,	2½" × 2½"	NA	35	NA	NA	11	35
143/I	BOOTS	6½"	NA	175	90	NA	55	175
150/0	HAPPY DAYS	5"	NA	175	NA	NA	58	175
150/I	HAPPY DAYS	6"	NA	250	NA	NA	109	225
151/W	MADONNA, SEATED W/CHILD	12"	NA	300	138	200	85	300
151/II		12"	NA	750	275	NA	200	750
153/I	AUF WIEDERSEHEN	7"	NA	250	98	NA	43	175
154/I	WAITER	7"	NA	225	95	NA	42	175
163	WHITSUNTIDE	7"	NA	350	99	NA	62	325

*During 1978 most of the reissues were available only in very limited quantities in Germany and Canada as shown in this list.

Note: These figures are based on extremely limited data with wide fluctuations. Use with that in mind.

CMP—Current Market Price (U.S. $, except Canada). SRP—Suggested Retail Price. NA—Not Available on Price List or Offered for Sale.

Number/ Size Mark	Name	Size	U.S.A.		CANADA		GERMANY	
			Low	High	Low	High	Low	High
165	PLQ Swaying Lullaby	5″ × 5″	NA	100	68	NA	34	75
167	HWF Angel w/Yellow Bird, or Sitting Angel	3″ × 4¾″	20	30	NA	NA	11	NA
168	PLQ Standing Boy	4″ × 5″	60	75	56	60	35	75
176/I	HAPPY BIRTHDAY	6″	NA	225	NA	NA	63	225
180	PLQ Tuneful Good Night,	5″ × 4¾″	NA	80	70	70	43	NA
183	FOREST SHRINE	9″	NA	425	205	NA	125	395
192	CAN Candlelight	6¾″	NA	150	68	NA	42	145
196/I	TELLING HER SECRET	6½″	NA	225	196	NA	110	225
206	Angel Cloud	2¼″ × 4¾″	20	100	NA	NA	NA	NA
218/0	BIRTHDAY SERENADE	5¼″	NA	175	80	100	49	175
M224/II	TLP Wayside Harmony	9½″	180	200	165	NA	100	NA
M225/II	TLP Just Resting	9½″	180	200	165	NA	100	NA
M231	TLP Birthday Serenade	9½″	200	225	125	NA	120	NA
M232	TLP Happy Days	9½″	200	225	185	NA	120	NA
M234	TLP Birthday Serenade	7½″	180	200	165	NA	100	NA
M235	TLP Happy Days	7½″	180	200	165	NA	100	NA
243	HWF Madonna and Child	3″ × 4″	20	25	NA	NA	10	NA
353/0	SPRING DANCE	5″	NA	300	98	NA	106	275
360/A	WVS Boy & Girl	6¼″	50	75	45	NA	28	NA
360/B	WVS Boy	6¼″	50	75	43	NA	26	NA
360/C	WVS Girl	6¼″	50	75	43	NA	26	NA

NOTES

These figures are based on a limited number of sources and are subject to wide swings as supply and demand change.

All reissues would be expected to have the recent Goebel trademark called V over E, TMK-5, although reports indicate that a few earlier marks may have been shipped.

As of press time no comprehensive comparison had been made of any visual differences between the old and new models other than the newer trademarks.

Illustrations of new and old Whitsuntide on page 60 show a difference in height and minor design variations.

Canadian Suggested Retail Prices exceed German ones by amounts ranging from 8 percent for Spring Dance, 353/0, to 100 percent more for Swaying Lullaby Plaque, 165. Most Canadian prices range from 50 to 60 percent higher than German prices.

Quantities of reissues are very limited compared to quantities of "regular" figurines shown in U.S. catalog for 1978.

TWO MORE REASONS TO INSURE HUMMEL COLLECTIONS*

A very small percentage of Hummel owners realize that the value of their collections has increased by 50 percent or more in the last twelve months. Even those with insurance are in a vulnerable position.

Prior to the book *Hummel Art* there was no authoritative information on which to base realistic appraisals. All that has changed. A survey of insurance companies that has just been completed shows conclusively that the large majority of insurors writing Fine Arts Policies will accept the descriptions and prices in *Hummel Art* and this *Supplement* as official values for your possessions and the basis for settlement in case of loss or breakage. No longer is an expensive appraisal by a second party necessary in most cases. Sometimes, this can mean a savings of several hundred dollars for the individual collector.

Talks with hundreds of Hummel owners during the past year have revealed a woeful lack of insurance coverage. For example, there were several owners of collections of fifty thousand dollars or more who had no coverage at all, and two owners with several fine old examples were covered for only a fraction of the value because they had only the retail price list to use. The phenomenal increase in the value of figurines makes insurance not only practical but advisable for persons owning even as few as five to ten pieces.

For those owners who still feel insurance is not worthwhile, a minimum program would be to list all their Hummel art by evaluating them as mentioned above. This list accompanied by photographs should be kept in a safety deposit box. For help in photographing any possessions send 35c to the Eastman Kodak Company, 343 State Street, Rochester, NY 14650, for a copy of "Photographs Help When Disaster Strikes."

DISCOVERY OF RARE AND UNUSUAL HUMMEL ITEMS IN 1978

On the back cover and on the following pages, of this *Supplement to Hummel Art* there are several exciting examples of Hummel art only recently reported. All of which indicates the potential of "Acres of Diamonds" that remain to be discovered by enterprising collectors.

Other interesting additions to Hummel knowledge which are not illustrated due to lack of available space are: Annual Plates for 1971 through 1978 in plain overglaze white and undecorated; a 1973 Annual Plate in white bisque finish, possibly an unfinished example; and Worship, 84, also in white overglaze, which has been exhibited. A rare example of Shrine Table Lamp, 100, was shown during the year. Delivery Angel, 301; Mother's Aid, 325; Naughty Boy, 326; and Birthday Wish, 338 have been displayed and may be prototypes of models to be released in the future. At least five variations of newspaper titles on Latest News, 184, have been reported. Old Wall Vases, 370A, B, and C are an interesting addition to one collection as are the unusual pair of Ba Bee Rings, 30 A and B, found in another collection, which have red rings instead of the usual white ones.

*See *Hummel Art*, pages 190-192 for essential background on this subject.

1. M. I. Hummel "Walking Stick" rubber doll, c. 1954.

2. M. I. Hummel "Chimney Sweep" rubber doll, c. 1954, with hat similar to figurine's.

3. M. I. Hummel "Chimney Sweep" doll with large, unusual hat.

4. MADONNA WITH CHILD, Hummel 151,
with blue cloak. Reissued in 1978 and incised
TMK-5, from the Dean collection.

5. Left, 1978 reissue of WHITSUNTIDE,
Hummel 163, 6½" high. At right, original
WHITSUNTIDE, TMK-2, 7" + high, from the
Dean collection.

6. Reproduction of HEAVENLY PROTEC-
TION, Hummel 88, with flowers instead of
basket in girl's right hand.

6A. Base of HEAVENLY PROTECTION
reproduction showing brushmarked S 441 iden-
tification.

7. Crystal version of GOOSE GIRL, Hummel 47, from the C. Goodwin collection.

8. Brooches inspired by Hummel figures. Made by Creed of North Attleboro, Maine.

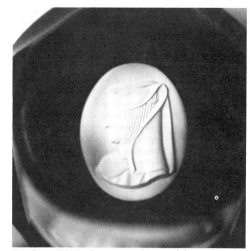

9.   Sister Maria Innocentia Hummel faceted
sulphide paperweight. Limited 1978 edition
produced by Schmid Bros.

10.   Smiling Through. 1979 Exclusive special
edition plaque for members of the Goebel
Collectors' Club.

11.   Angel Light, Hummel 241. Available
but not cataloged in 1978. $10^{3/8}''$ x $8^{3/8}''$.

REVISIONS OF SOURCES*

Auctioneers

Delete - **L. Sones, Auctioneer**

Change- **Lufkins** *to*
4301 Cat Mountain Drive
Austin, Texas 78731
Bid by mail auctions, only.

Add - **Pace & Albert Auctioneers**
Route 2 Box 64
Ivanhoe, Illinois 60060
312-949-0330

Dealers-U.S.A.

Delete - **Dorothy's Treasures**
Danish Imports, Inc.
Sam F. Jackson
Shirley Ann-Tiques

Change- **Carol's Gift Shop** *to*
retail only, no mail order
Pat Arbenz *to*
Misty's Gift Gallery
205 Fry Blvd.
Sierra Vista, Arizona 85635
602-458-7208
Ruth Laudien *to*
432 Palmetto Dr.
Lake Park, Florida 33403
Mader's Collector's Gift Shop *to*
1037 N. 3rd St.
Milwaukee, Wisconsin 53204
414-271-1911
Old Towne Colonial Center *to*
16960 N. Meadow Lane
Strongsville, Ohio 44126
Scottsdale East *to*
Ron Heberlee
8011 East Roosevelt
Scottsdale, Arizona 85275
Mail order, mainly old Hummels.

Add - **Eileen Grande**
12 Iroquois Drive
Saratoga Springs, New York 12866
518-584-1763
Buys and sells new and old figurines.
Grandma's Gallery
12957 Gulf Blvd. East
Madiera Beach, Florida 33707
813-393-2777
Buys and sells new and old figurines.
Donna L. Pokorn
Route 2 Box 250Z
Chicamauga Lane
Long Grove, Illinois
Buys and sells new and old figurines.
Maxine's Limited
6575 University
Des Moines, Iowa 50311

Dealers-Foreign

Delete - **Das Kleine Hummel Haus**
Aa Hyldgaard
Scanmark
R.F. Sowinski
Add - **Lucette**
Postfach 1169
6367 Korben
West Germany
Sells new and old Hummels to
collectors and dealers by mail.

Shanfield and Meyer
Ouellette Street
Windsor, Canada
U.S. phone - 313-961-8435
Sells new Hummels by mail.

Display-Suppliers

Delete - **Century Display Manufacturing Corp.**

Insurance

Add - **Huntington T. Block**
2101 L Street N.W.
Washington, D.C. 20037
800-424-8830
Fine Arts insurance specialist.

* Refer to pages 209-221 in Hummel Art.